TRANSIT

TRANSIT

Niloofar Fanaiyan

TRANSIT
Recent Work Press
Canberra, Australia

Copyright © Niloofar Fanaiyan, 2016

National Library of Australia
Cataloguing-in-Publication entry.

Fanaiyan, Niloofar

Transit/ Niloofar Fanaiyan

ISBN:9780994456564(paperback)

A821.4

All rights reserved. This book is copyright. Except for private study, research, criticism or reviews as permitted under the Copyright Act, no part of this book may be reproduced stored in a retrieval system, or transmitted in any form by any means without prior written permission. Enquiries should be addressed to the publisher.

Cover illustration: 'Return flight, CPH-STO' (2015) by Jack Wallsten reproduced under Creative Commons attribution licence 2.0

Insert adapted from 'Mono Bird' (2016) by Johnathan Meddings reproduced under Creative Commons attribution licence 2.0

Farsi translation by Niloofar Fanaiyan

Cover design: Recent Work Press
Set in Sabon by Recent Work Press

recentworkpress.com

Contents

Leaving	9
Chasing stories	10
Secrets of salt	13
Red film	16
In a many-layered cotton sling	18
Goodbye	20
On the way	21
Window 1	22
Flying over Tabriz	23
Window 2	24
I remember the day I was born…	25
The luggage was packed	27
On the periphery 1	28
Arrivals	29
Waiting	30
Beyond midnight…	31
Song of the Caravan	32
In Transit	35
Winter	36
Possibilities 1	37
Reunion	38
Finding	40

365 days	42
'Meet me at the airport'	43
Reveal	44
On the Periphery 2	45
In the garden	47
That song	48
And then it was gone	49
Weaving	51
Possibilities 2	52
The castle wall	53
Detour	54
The morning star	55
Salt and cucumber	56
The last three hours	58
Two hours before sunset	59
The final hour	60
Pomegranates	61
Notes	64
Acknowledgements	65

Leaving

Write a to-do list

Pack for all weathers

Don't forget the camera (and three lenses)

Remember to say goodbye

Hide the key

Chasing stories

The first letter ensnared me, like a child
grabs your hand eagerly to run to play,
the first letter of the first word unfurled
my mind like a magnolia
at daybreak, bade me follow the streams
of sound and thought and light—

I ran till the end of the word, the child
beckoned from beyond the hill,
the second word gleaming in his eye,
the letters of the second word fell
against my skin like rain unnoticed but for the second letter,
a drop of rain on parched paper—

I ran till I was on the train, the child

beside me smiled,

the words blurred against the window

of old textured paper and thin flowing ink

became a web of laughter of longing of tears

descending through my mind—

the train slowed lurching the light, the child

looked expectantly at the door behind,

I grabbed his hand and we ran

to chase another story.

دل ای رفیق درین کاروانسرای مبند
که خانه ساختن آیین کاروانی نیست

Your heart, oh friend, do not bind to this caravanserai,

For the building of houses is not the practice of caravans.

From Ghasideh #8, *Bustan*, Saadi

Secrets of salt

دل به دل راه دارد

*Del be del rah darad—
hearts lead to hearts (an
old Persian proverb)*

through the skies,

water fowl fly in formation

    over hills and plains,

past my window of four squares

through which I see but cannot touch

the gradual mutation of colour on the horizon,

the disappearance of birds beyond the blue line,

smattering of stars blending into night lights

against faint echoes of the warbling

بلبل و عطر گلاب،

*Bolbol o atr e golab—
nightingales and the
perfume of rose-water*

    winding through time—

      a diaspora searching,

multitudes crawling backwards through the snow—

geometric patterns of blue and red appear

on two squares of window

(not out of place considering the crawling and cold),

    the

برف و یخ که به استخوان میچسبد
ولی گرمای دل را از بین نمیبرد.
گفته اند دل به دل راه دارد

Barf o yakh ke be ostoghan michasbad valy garmhaye del ra az bein nemibarad. Gofte and del be del rah darad—snow and ice that sticks to the bones but does not destroy the warmth of the heart. They say hearts lead to hearts

across oceans and on separate lands

we stand on sandy beaches,

mottled by the one moonlight,

shadowed by memories of

لبهای مادر بر پیشانی فرزند،

Labhaye madar bar pishounye farzand—lips of a mother on the forehead of a child

our tongues taste the salt of tears

of generations of earth and water,

as waves that once washed over your feet

approach the leaning palm trees where I stand.

I hear many voices speak;

دستم را بگیر، چشمها را ببند،
دل به دل راه دارد

Dastam ra begir, chashmha ra beband, del be del rah darad—
take my hand, close your eyes,
hearts lead to hearts

as we dig deeper into the ground

searching for the earth's subconscious

seeking the collective heart—

the darker soil yields its secrets,

its star-made particles—

    souls lead to souls

    thoughts lead to thoughts

    hearts lead to hearts —

دل به دل راه دارد،

Del be del rah darad—hearts lead to hearts

hearts lead to hearts

Red film

Yellow light streams

through cloud—

collides with the air

of dust—

a curtain of sunbeams

shifts on the horizon.

The engine groans

brown foliage flies

insects crash onto the windscreen

the curtain breaks

dry earth invades cavities.

A thunderclap;

three fat drops

renew a hopeless longing.

The smell of mud

storms through the window

or perhaps it is a dream

that meddles with my senses.

Over the hill

and now more meddling—

dust is mingling with

scores of *pieris rapae*,

the frenetic fluttering

of fragile white wings

leads our labouring vehicle

down a road of red clay.

And in the distance

a green garden

and beyond the garden

a green field—

leaves lightly stained by

brown and red film,

still mixing in the wind.

In a many-layered cotton sling

This was never meant to be our home
we rented four walls and a patch of soil
taught ourselves the local language
drank from the village well
till a warm current came down from the mountain
and stirred the wings of silence—

we packed our hearts in a homespun purse,
primed the feathers with thyme and lavender,
left our songs by the last door
left our paintings by the last window
curled up in a sling of many layered cotton
and submitted to the wings of silence—

silence carried us far but far was near

silence made space for spinning, cleared

the canvas for drawing more dreams, silence

was when we remembered our prayers,

when we wrote new songs and sang

a warm current beneath the wings of silence.

Goodbye
for M.S.

We parted at the threshold with *Khodahafiz*—a heartfelt prayer that God would keep us till we next meet. The crowds rushed around us as though around an island in the rapids, elbows and luggage brushing and jarring on their way. You said you would miss 'our long conversations' and I said 'over tea'. I said I would miss 'our long walks' and you said 'on the hills behind the city'. Now I gaze out an oval frame at the 'sun-drenched hills', clusters of lilac wild-flowers dotting the verdure, and it is as though you are sitting beside me as the cart squeezes through the aisles, as the smell of bergamot gets confused with cardamom, as a trickle of cold air from the vents reminds me of a sea-breeze, as the oval frame takes the place of your kitchen window, as the warmth of the sunlight replaces the warmth of your smile, and the closing of eyes marks a heartfelt prayer—*Khodahafiz*.

On the way

Drink plenty of fluids

Learn your neighbour's name

Note the snoring patterns,

the shift in altitude

Compose a song about flying (out loud)

Window 1

The cat's green eyes stare back at me through the oval window, his white paws disappear into precipitation. His fur blazes in the sunset—spontaneous combustion is possible when material is positioned above clouds— as the captain announces 'we expect some turbulence', the child in 16A cries, stabbing a chubby finger at the glass, points at Ginger— felines in a far-off land lift their faces heavenward. The green eyes turn blue then dark blue then black as the seatbelt sign turns off.

Flying over Tabriz
for M.F.

We fly over it every time,

and every time 'time' slows

as we pass over—

it pulls us   the land a lodestone   the eye of our compass.

City lights far below signal sleepy households

unaware of our passage outside. We skirt

its invisible lines—its mountains taller

and its borders wider every time, and every time

we are turned away.

The spirits' voices grow louder

and you and I grow quieter

as we pass over

holy land   tortured land   suffering land

The caravan does not rest tonight,

neither do our prayers.

Window 2

Soft rivulets of pastel sunlit caramel course between ice and charcoal. The mountains fall away into lakes of soft misty clouds—vales of dreams—hiding worlds within, at the bottom of those lakes. White and grey ripples brush up against the edges of the lake-shore and disappear into the blue horizon. The smell of coffee and butter mingles with dust whooshing through the air system. Flight paths make long lines in the lake surface—dolphins of the sky—the wing light flashes orange just above the yellow line.

I remember the day I was born…

…standing at the gate a new passport to my nose, the smell of the pages overwhelming and distracting from frenetic movement in the hall—as we trudged forward windows would crack and shatter in our wake, the ground shook and bounced and rolled and we did not know whether the plane took off or the earth had flung the plane to the sky. It was years before we paused on a sandy beach with warm water washing along the shore, red cliffs in the distance sharp and forbidding, tall palm trees leaning east leaning towards the place I was born—the light weight of a lead pencil in my hand, I tried to capture the ocean in shapes in colours in words, knowing I might never return. We stopped many times after the beach, no place more vivid than another, no name more musical, no zephyr more moving, but the growing warmth of the sun's fingertips caressing the flesh of my palms caressing the lines and veins of my days, and the oscillating voice in the fading starlight chants 'remember the day you were born'.

کاروان رفت و تو در خواب و بیابان در پیش
وه که بس بی‌خبر از غلغل چندین جرسی

The caravan has departed and you remain asleep and the desert lies before you,

Oh how is it that you remain unaware of the jingling of the many camel bells.

From Ghazal #455, *Divan*, Hafiz

The luggage was packed

It took at least two suitcases to carry one person,
six to carry three—
if only the people were lighter, the bags could be
spread out more.
And the people handlers—
they had to make sure the people would not
get wet, or damaged, or lost,
or sent on detour—
a person on detour was a sight to behold,
their luggage waiting for them on the other side
while they stood amidst the dust gazing
at a snow-capped horizon.
The luggage was packed,
and ready for new holding rooms, ready
to be worn down, slowly,
from border to border, from coast to coast,
perhaps shedding a person or two
along the way.

On the periphery 1

Eat

Visit one landmark per day

Breathe the sea air

Breathe the night lights

Eat again

Arrivals

…how long will she stand there, waiting—I've seen that look before—the slightly wider eyes, the pursed lips, the tilt of the head, as she stares past the sparse forest of pillars, the river of people winding their way through customs, the increasing light casting notes of confusion on resin-coated floors, the flow of the river fluctuates as planes land intermittently, the gates swing wider, the gears in the clock tick faster, the fading pallor of her skin the cold artificial air weariness in her limbs many colours many thoughts through her mind through her body through her waiting—she is still standing there, waiting…

Waiting

The fraying bag strap digs into her
left shoulder. She stands at the gate,
it's past midnight on a summer's eve—
the clicking, ticking, clicking
of little wheels over white tiles,
the smell of leather and metal and twenty
discordant perfumes,
a hectic, in-between space—
time seems to stop and run away.
It's a waiting game in a nameless place—
what is she waiting for?

Beyond midnight...

...we lose track of the time difference in the dark in the light in the half-light, as we weave ourselves through a kaleidoscope of dreams and awakenings, threads of seconds ticking over against ragged cliffs, in tandem with ocean currents, skimming the tall grass and then the sandy dunes, synchronous with the flashing of stars that guide us through wispy clouds through the thin air through the night beneath the glowing loom—we lose track of the time difference in borders in hemispheres in layovers, where longing and struggle and hope are the colours of our weaving, a tapestry of memory as the future and the future as memory, where a mother's voice has not yet been heard and a child's voice was born yesterday, where intricate lilies mark the corners and edges of time, the subtle scent of them tugging on our breath on our tears, wafting into morning into midday into night beyond midnight...

Song of the Caravan

مرغ سحر ناله را در سینه حبس کرد
آسمان اشک ریخت و زمین سر بلند کرد

Morghe sahar nale ra dar seene habs kard, aseman ashk reekht o zameen sar boland kard— the rooster kept his call buried in his chest, the sky wept and the earth raised her head

to face the morning star and taste

her sorrow-filled tears from eyes that see

too much—the rooster's feathers ruffled by rain

he rests his head on damp soil,

and listens to sounds of a caravan missed

tracing paths of mud into the distance.

A little girl crouches by the red bricks

of a caravanserai, her shadow crouches

by the red bricks in the corner, watching

as she comforts the rooster. Her fingertips

are pale and numb from hunger, dry lines

tracing the backs of her hands—

زخم دل بر پوست رو شد،
زخم پوست بر سایه رو شد،

Zakhme del bar poost roo shod, zakhme poost bar sayeh roo shod— the heart's wound appeared on skin, the skin's wound appeared on shadow and her shadow sees explosions in the distance,

feels the ground tremble, the ground trembles then

shakes, dust falling from bricks onto her shadow

از پشت پرده پیدا نشد غم دل،
دل صبور ماند منتظر ساربان دل

Az poshte pardeh peyda nashod ghame del, dele saboor mand montazere sareban del— the heart's sorrow was hidden behind a veil, the patient heart remained waiting for its sareban

last night they told her to stay and wait

before they disappeared into the dark

but last night was a thousand years ago,

the birds have flown but for the rooster,

the walls have crumbled but for her wall,

and a curtain of rain tries to hide her from her shadow

مرغ سحر به سایه پر و بال داد،
آرزوی خورشید ترانهٔ امید داد

Morghe sahar be sayeh par o bal dad, arezooye khorshid taranehye omid dad— the rooster gave feathers and wings to shadow, desire of the sun gave a song of hope

his feathers become many shades of turquoise

as they both lift their heads

at the sound of bells approaching, bells becoming

louder than war, loud like the burgeoning light—

ای ساربان سحر،
درود بر آن چهرهٔ نور افشان،
بر آن آغوش رنگین کمان،
رنگ به رنگ شد راه به راه شد نغمهٔ آن کاروان

and this time she is ready, standing at the gate, girl and shadow and bird are one.

Ey sarebane sahar, dorood bar an chehreye noor-afshan, bar an aghooshe rangeen-kamaan, rang be rang shod rah be rah shod naghmeye an karevaan— Oh caravan driver of the dawn, greetings upon your radiant face, upon your rainbow-like embrace, colour to colour became paths to paths became the song of the caravan

In Transit

Staying still when everything else is moving around you, like trying to keep your bearings on the deck of a ship in the middle of a storm, or trying to sit in the midst of a bustling crowd, or being a gear incarnate stuck at the centre of a perpetual motion machine— it is possible to remain in the same spot for too long— the flow of your blood slows, muscles begin to twitch with forgetfulness, pauses and rests lose their meaning, and the movement of melodies flat-line— even cemeteries refuse to be static— the stones change colour, cracks appear, flowers grow, bloom, wither, fade, then grow again— and in the midst of remaining still a white butterfly floats and flutters across your peripheral vision, then alights on the curve of your left shoulder.

Winter

'When will you return?'

you ask,

icy wind whipping my scarf between us, slithering

between fabric and skin, into pores. Your question

is the chill seeping into my bones. Your eyes

widen stretching the silence; the train

moves faster and farther away stretching

the distance; cold dissipates, warmer weather stretching

my skin and sinews.

The smell of damp decaying foliage meanders through the carriage

as we pass through an ancient land,

my phone buzzing with your latest endearment—

a picture of snowfall. But the snow

only reminds me of the icy wind

the chill in my bones

the desire to stretch this distance into an invisible thread— there is no going backwards

on these tracks.

'When will you return?'

you ask.

Possibilities 1

Attempt to speak in the local language

                                                                               Smile

Stay silent and attempt sign language

                                 Speak boldly in your own language

                                        Avoid all communication

Reunion

I see them there as I walk through the doors—
how many moments have I spent
seeing this moment, feeling lifted above movement,
      a tangential spindle in the gyrations—
      my heart is close at hand—

They smile in the reflections of still water,
wide-stretching rivers at rest,
resting from winding explorations,
      an invitation to camp by the banks—
      my mind strolls over the hills—

They walk by my side in dark windows
dark edges blurring with antiques
covered in faded scenes of reunion,
      overlayed by great landmarks
      orbiting my other side—

bridges, locks, and towers pass,

    countries break,

    rain stops, falls, stops again—

I have become movement and non-movement—

I see them there as I walk through the doors.

Finding

Postcard in my pocket,
some letters are harder to write—
before you arrive clouds
line up for a display of moods,
greenery sparkles like moss in a rainforest, rain
washes cobblestones till they gleam,
concentrations of cold light—

postcard on the table,
'Dearest' sits at the top—
it's not in the city but in the people
in the city, the fluttering
that accompanies laughter,
an upright gait, the warm smell of garlic and butter,
I long for that warmth
but the fire is closed—

postcard waiting beneath my hand,

'I think I may have found it' I start,

airport post-boxes look suspiciously unused—

the sea is many shades of blue,

rooftops are the beige of a nearby desert,

the mountain murmurs to me— I murmur to you—

remember how I once carried

postcards in my pocket.

365 days

It was all light,
>   many shades of light, a shape
without lines or borders, but
>   defined by temperature, like being
stranded on the tip of an ice-berg,
>   floating on a sun-drenched cloud,
pert sourness of lemon sorbet,
>   sticky sweetness of a marshmallow—
It constantly writhed and roiled, a hidden
>   sun surrounded by flesh
of many layers of many textures,
>   drawing us all inevitably
closer— it moves below us
>   and through space, and we
continue oblivious, travelling
>   back and forth while it carries us
on a greater journey.

'Meet me at the airport'

You run down the corridors,

along the travelators,

your mind is mist-laden with the lingering effects of sleep

as you dodge the caravan of seven

with their fourteen items of luggage.

You run past Gate twelve—

eleven gates to go.

The words on the screens alternate, *Departures, Arrivals, Departures,*

Your nostrils twitch at the smell of coffee

but you dare not pause this time.

You run through a pseudo-lobby,

slide past the American Express stand,

and halt before a tide of people moving in different phases.

You study the face waiting at the counter—

Is it him?

Reveal

Curtains of daylight draw to reveal the universe— I remain near the pillar by the power socket, leaning my cheek against the cool window, peering around reflections in the glass, looking for your figure on the tarmac— three days later the curtains are half drawn when I think it is your plane that lands, a canvas of autumn twilight beyond the runways— a slight girl nudges my arm as she crouches to recharge her phone, sends a spark of static through woollen polyester through flesh, 'are you waiting for the flight from Neyshabur?' she asks, she taps the screen over and over again, 'its three days late' she says and continues to tap the screen— a blanket screaming, an older woman paces the hall with a crying baby in her arms, the baby blanket is turquoise, like the turquoise bracelet you found in the market— another plane lands but you do not appear, the curtain is gone again, 'attention please, attention…' static speakers— blanket static— half the lights go out— and this time I can't avoid the reflection— the window is filled with me.

On the Periphery 2

Search for hyacinths,

their delicate fragrance will lead you to the field—

and if there are no hyacinths then frangipani will do,

(they are both sweet-smelling flowers)

tuck a flower behind your ear

then tiptoe around the crowd.

کاروان آمد و دلخواه به همراهش نیست
با دل این قصه نگویم که به دلخواهش نیست
کاروان آمد و از یوسف من نیست خبر
این چه راهیست که بیرون شدن از چاهش نیست

The caravan has arrived and my beloved is not amongst the travellers,

I will not tell my heart this tale for my heart cannot bear it.

The caravan has arrived and there is no news of my 'Joseph',

What path has it taken that found no way out of the well?

From #26, *Ghazal*, Shahriar

In the garden

Waiting

                as though waiting at the turn of the season,

like jacaranda blossoms high above,

        hovering amongst their verdant and feathery nest,

waiting for the strongest wind

                      to direct

                                    their

                                              fall.

That song

In darkness I fear the end of darkness, the pause, the appearance of calm, silence before the fall. In darkness little sounds become chaos and cacophony, skin and dust, hair and water, I become one with the earth and it is bitter-sweet. In darkness I dream that you are a star, I try to measure the echoes of light that surround you, waves of warmth, like burnished autumn leaves floating onto my lap in the winking afternoon sun. In darkness I remain the earth, still but spinning at the same time - the stars are shedding that song again - there are no words for the rest of it.

And then it was gone

I.
Her eyelids fall softly
till upper lashes whisper against lower lashes—
the bell drops—
that moment she feels the warm encasing of eyes
she knows it is too late—
blinking is perilous in the sunshine.

II.
She blinks, tears in the corner of her eye,
clinging to the soft curve of her cheeks like drops
of sun-shower sliding against a sunlit window.
She never notices how many times
the doors open and close.

III.

Smoke, heavy-laden with eucalypt

surrounds him, the oily leaves burning,

lightening a heavy soul—

an easterly wind stirs the fragrant fumes—

he blinks—lashes mingle with lashes—

the night is gone, and so is the static—

he blinks and blinks again.

Weaving

They say the caravan travels to Sistan

bearing a treasury of silk, winding its way as silken

thread through the woollen canvas of desert,

the Sareban a steady pilot following

the tendrils of light that shoot out

over the eastern horizon—

flying home we pass over

Sistan with its store-houses of silk

and move beyond the horizon, beyond

the gleaming sunrise, bearing

few treasures and fewer gifts,

but laden with memories that cling like silk

worms to the leaves of the mind—they consume

time in a space where there is no time,

and afterwards leave silken

shells that unravel and weave

through the breath before.

Possibilities 2

Take photographs worthy of National Geographic

                                                    Leave the camera in the camera bag

Send out updates every few hours

                                                             Keep it all a surprise

                                        Sit on the edge and watch the sun rise

The castle wall

at the airport again it's hard to say goodbye again over and over again
   will this pattern climb the walls like wild roses

we hug once and part
fingers linger at the elbow, bodies half turn
but turn back refusing to let go
a woollen cardigan caught on the thorns

catch the corner and it begins
to unravel our sense of belonging
and not belonging—we are
everywhere and nowhere
we hug once more, tears
touch faces, touch roses leaning
away from the castle wall
but you turn towards the tunnel

a lengthening thread dangles

as the pattern climbs higher and higher as you whisper goodbye again
   and again at the airport

Detour

A detour was announced—
'we will be turning left at Mars'—
A young man with six different devices
stirred 'if it was up to me we would
head straight for Antares',
the nun called Bridget rolled her eyes
'Spica is safest, I was told so in a dream',
a man with three small children leaned
over the back of his chair 'Hadar
will have the most diverse planets', a little girl
noisily slurped her orange juice.
I tried to ignore her and focus
on the diversion at hand—
the captain appeared
displeased with the raucousness,
captain's hat and beard both
missing, 'we are going to Mimosa'—
I dropped my phone.

The morning star

You were almost forgotten—

when they consigned you to the morning sky (to hover above the increasing girth of a yellow line) to watch over flickering street lamps and Calpurnia stirring in fitful sleep, to guide those racked with insomnia back to the wash basin and a splash of cold water, when they placed you on a pedestal (discounting nausea and vertigo) and kept you far from your children from your lovers from your kind, when cracked lips murmured your name in hot tears and in hot blood, when they chose to misunderstand you, your thoughts, your affections, your oddly tilted smile, when they spread rumours and satires wrenching the pedestal away but leaving you in that vast darkness your breath barely making it past the atmosphere to touch what remained of your story—Venus—

and yet your light remained, a bright lodestone in an oval window, before the sunrise.

Salt and cucumber

She entered his life with salt and cucumber—
the light minerally smell as she bit
into the fruit wafted across the aisle,
carried him to his uncle's garden
on a hot summer day, she paused
to sprinkle some salt
over the pale green flesh then
turned to look at him, 'would you like one?'
his eyes widened slightly—

'help me finish them, we can't take them
through customs you know' and she handed over
a fresh little cucumber with a tiny packet of salt—
two rough hands broke
the cucumber in half, a soft crunch sounded,
drops of bitter liquid dripped
into the soil below, it was dark
and overly warm, crickets chirped
in a deep pitch from two rows back—

'they're from my mother's garden' her voice

echoed in the cabin, two grains of salt

lingered on her lower lip like

two lost stars—he looked up

at his uncle with pursed lips, a little more salt would

hide the bitterness, would

alter the soil would

alter the cricket song and

the stars on her lips—

the wind picked up speed,

and he asked for another cucumber.

The last three hours

I walk up and down

the length   of the cabin.

The people of a suspended world

sleep   at apogee.

I stretch my arms   up and   out

to the sides   and pretend   to fly

over the gently nodding heads,

murmuring songs to keep myself awake.

There are no witnesses

at forty thousand feet.

Two hours before sunset

Feel your heart beating in your chest, the blood crawling through veins, the tingle on skin as the air moves slightly, as soft arms of afternoon sunlight reach out and caress your eyes, your eyes see everything as radiant particles – whispered prayers echo within and without as though you stand at the heart of an amphitheatre, a domed cathedral, a cave, and the cave is the world with no beginning and no end – your myriad of questions grow arms grow legs and eventually wings with curious tips, they trip and dance and fly away, chasing the sunset chasing the corners of the cave – just as the echoes fade into crevices voices descend in a torrent of decibels to enter through fingers and toes – the answers to your questions move through blood into heart, lodged within your self.

The final hour

There is only one hour left. And should I be surprised, since all moments must come to an end—the moment of flight, the moment of rest moment of anguish of joy of release, sharp licks of a hot sun burning the curve of a shoulder, shock of cold oceanic waves lapping against warm skin, bubbles of laughter bursting from the mouth of a toddler, voices of loving chatter of quiet regret unrestrained longing and again—there is only one hour left. And I am not surprised. And yet allow me to live this moment forever, to know these sensations in waking, in dreaming, fingers stretching towards horizons, colours dragging at the corner of my eye, begging me to follow to leap to surrender to soar, and to cry in the knowledge—there is only one hour left.

Pomegranates

Where is the world that I seek?

I move through four seasons—

the warm wind winks and turns,

a spell of cold air infusing its dance,

the flushed husk breaks open to reveal

ruby drops, tears of autumn—

bitter   sour   sweet

I collect the gemstones and wonder how long they will last.

از چندین سرزمین گذشتم،
از ستاره به ستاره، از نور به نور،
تا بین دو کهکشان حیران ماندم——

Az chandin sarzamin gozashtam, az setareh be setareh, az noor be noor, ta beine do kahkeshan heyran mandam— I passed many lands, from star to star, from light to light, till between two galaxies I paused, perplexed—

If I move through the world that I seek, move

in the world that I cannot explain,

how will I recognise the

فصلهای بلند و فصلهای کوتاه،
دریای قطره و قطرۀ دریا؟

faslhaye boland va faslhaye kootah, daryaye ghatreh va ghatrehye darya— long seasons and short seasons, oceans of drops and a drop of ocean?

Winter is filled with birdsong, seeming to answer

the grey weariness with a lively timbre.

The wind begins to turn again with the turn of light—

frost in the distance— frosty sand shifting,

stardust across the night—

A gemstone falls from my purse,

breaks and spills red through the sand,

bitter   sour   sweet

sings

جرس زندگی بر خاک زیر پا،
ببین که دنیا منم و منم دنیا

Jarase zendegy bar khake zeere pa, bebin ke donya manam va manam donya— the bells of life lie on the dust beneath your feet, see how the world is me and I am the world

The liquid continues as it dissipates,

ringing softly into the dawn. I hold the purse

of rubies high, then spill the tears onto the sand—

red becomes brown becomes black—

black as the beginning of the world.

And now we start again.

Notes

Tabriz—a city in the north west of Iran where The Bab, prophet-herald of the Bahá'i Faith, and scores of his followers were martyred in the 19th century CE.

Morghe sahar—literally translates as 'dawn bird' and is a reference to the title of a popular song written by Moḥammad-Taqi Bahār and Morteżā Ney-Dāwud in the early 19th century CE. The song is both a lament and an incitement to hope and action.

Neyshabur—a city in the north east of Iran, was a major stop on the old Silk Road, famous for its turquoise mines, and was the city of the mystical Sufi poet Attar.

Hyacinths—are the flowers that are typically incorporated into traditional Persian Naw Ruz decorations. They are an important signifier of the coming of spring and new beginnings.

Sistan—a region in the east of Iran and a reference to a famous qasideh, written by Farrukhi Sistani around 1000 CE called 'With a Caravan of Fine Robes'/

با کاروان حله

Sareban—is the title of the caravan driver or head of the caravan.

Acknowledgements

A version of the poem 'In Transit' has previously appeared in *Otoliths*, Issue Forty-one.

Sincere thanks to friends and colleagues without whom this book would not be possible – members of my Wednesday night writers group (Gina Wyatt, Penny O'Hara, Kristin Milton, Jo Virgona, Kelly Muller) for providing constant encouragement, editorial genius, and a never-ending supply of tea—members of the IPSI Prose Poetry Project for receiving and providing a constantly revolving platform of prose poems—Paul Munden for inviting me to present the 'caravan paper' at Poetry on the Move (in which some of these poems appeared)—Alice Beecham for her insightful comments—Jen Crawford for reading my poetry and encouraging me onwards—Shane Strange for reading, editing, encouraging, and believing in the project.

I would like to thank my sister Melodi and my parents Farideh and Masoud for providing a house full of poetry and song, for reading and proof-reading, and for believing in me—this book is for you.

About the author

Having lived and worked in the U.S., the Netherlands, and Tanzania, Niloofar Fanaiyan currently lives in Canberra, Australia where she has recently completed a PhD in creative writing at the University of Canberra. She writes poetry and short fiction. *Transit* is her first book of poetry.

More Recent Work

Owen Bullock	*Urban Haiku (2015)* *River's Edge (2016)*
Paul Hetherington	*Gallery of Antique Art (2016)*
Niloofar Fanaiyan	*Transit (2016)*
Prose Poetry Project	*Seam (2015)* *Pulse (2016)*
Jen Webb	*Sentences from the Archive (2016)*
Monica Carroll, Jen Crawford, Owen Bullock & Shane Strange	*5 6 7 8 (2016)*
Subhash Jaireth	*Incantations (2016)*
Shane Strange	*Notes to the Reader (2015)*

all titles available from
recentworkpress.com

www.ingramcontent.com/pod-product-compliance
Lightning Source LLC
Chambersburg PA
CBHW022229010526
44113CB00033B/778